OBSOLETE

The Syracuse Orange®

BY
MARK STEWART

Content Consultant
Matt Zeysing
Historian and Archivist
The Naismith Memorial Basketball Hall of Fame

NORWOOD HOUSE 🏠 PRESS
CHICAGO, ILLINOIS

Norwood House Press
P.O. Box 316598
Chicago, Illinois 60631

For information regarding Norwood House Press, please visit our website at:
www.norwoodhousepress.com or call 866-565-2900.

All photos courtesy of Getty Images except the following:
Author's Collection (6, 37 top left, 40), Associated Press (17, 18, 19, 24, 26, 29),
The Post-Standard (7, 9, 31, 36 right, 41 both), Louis Rich, Inc. (14, 21, 25, 37 top right),
Syracuse University (16, 36 left, 37 bottom), Topps, Inc. (22), TCMA Ltd. (38),
Eastern Basketball Magazine (39).
Cover Photo: Associated Press/Kevin Rivoli

Special thanks to Topps, Inc.

Editor: Mike Kennedy
Designer: Ron Jaffe
Project Management: Black Book Partners, LLC.
Editorial Production: Jessica McCulloch
Research: Joshua Zaffos
Special thanks to Frank Radell

Library of Congress Cataloging-in-Publication Data

Stewart, Mark, 1960-
   The Syracuse Orange / by Mark Stewart ; content consultant, Matt
Zeysing.
       p. cm. -- (Team spirit--college basketball)
   Includes bibliographical references and index.
   Summary: "Presents the history and accomplishments of The Syracuse
University Orange basketball team. Includes highlights of players, coaches,
and awards, longstanding rivalries, quotes, timeline, maps, glossary, and
website"--Provided by publisher.
   ISBN-13: 978-1-59953-377-3 (library edition : alk. paper)
   ISBN-10: 1-59953-377-4 (library edition : alk. paper)
   1. Syracuse Orange (Basketball team)--Juvenile literature. 2. Syracuse
University--Basketball--Juvenile literature. I. Zeysing, Matt. II. Title.
   GV885.43.S95S74 2010
   796.323'630974766--dc22
                                                   2010004361

Manufactured in the United States of America in North Mankato, Minnesota.
159N—072010

COVER PHOTO: Syracuse fans pack the Carrier Dome for a 2007 game.

Table of Contents

SPORTS WORDS & VOCABULARY WORDS: In this book, you will find many words that are new to you. You may also see familiar words used in new ways. The glossary on page 46 gives the meanings of basketball words, as well as "everyday" words that have special basketball meanings. These words appear in **bold type** throughout the book. The glossary on page 47 gives the meanings of vocabulary words that are not related to basketball. They appear in ***bold italic type*** throughout the book.

Meet the Orange

The central part of New York State has played an important part in the history of basketball. For more than 100 years, it has had some of the sport's best teams and most creative players. The heart of the region's hoops territory is Syracuse University.

Syracuse players and coaches always find a way to get the most out of their talent. The Orange have a *tradition* of putting great teams on the court year after year. In fact, most of the fans at Syracuse games cannot remember the last time the Orange had a losing season!

This book tells the story of the Orange. They are fast, smart, and athletic. If opponents want to run, the Orange will outrun them. If the game turns into a "shootout," the Orange will outscore them. If things get a little rough under the basket, the Orange will play that game, too. That is why, on game night in Syracuse, Orange is more than just a team name—it's the color of victory.

Hakim Warrick dunks during a 2004 game. Syracuse has a great history of finding talented players like him.

Way Back When

Syracuse put its first basketball team on the court in 1900, just a few years after the sport was invented. The school originally called its teams the Orangemen because of its color. In 2004, the school changed to the Orange.

In the early 1900s, Syracuse had one of the best players in the country. His name was Art Powell. As a teenager, he played center for the Buffalo Germans, America's finest **amateur** basketball team at the

time. Powell helped bring several of his former teammates to Syracuse. Another talented center, Joe Schwarzer, made the Orangemen the top college team during the 1917–18 season.

Syracuse's 1925–26 team went 19–1 and was crowned the national champion. The captain of that squad was Vic Hanson. He was a great **all-around** athlete who broke every school scoring record. Hanson and teammates Gotch Carr and Charlie Lee were known as the "Three Musketeers." After they graduated, many more top players wore the team's orange uniform. That list included Ev Katz, Ed Sonderman, and Billy Gabor. In 1956–57, Vinnie Cohen led Syracuse to the national tournament of the **National Collegiate Athletic Association (NCAA)** for the first time.

During the 1960s, Syracuse went through ups and downs. But when Dave Bing joined the Orangemen, the team rose to new heights. Bing was an amazing player. In 1965–66, he led Syracuse in scoring, rebounds, and **assists**. That season, Syracuse just missed becoming the first school in history to average 100 points a game.

Syracuse reached the **Final Four** for the first time in 1974–75. It was one of seven trips the team made to the **NCAA Tournament** during the 1970s. In 1978–79, Roosevelt Bouie and Louis Orr formed the "Bouie & Louie Show" and led the Orangemen to a 26–4 record. The following season, Syracuse was one of the schools that came together to form The **Big East Conference**.

LEFT: A pin from the early days of Syracuse basketball.
ABOVE: Louis Orr releases a jump shot.

The coach who led Syracuse to its greatest success was Jim Boeheim. He played for the Orangemen in the 1960s and took over on the sidelines in 1976. From 1980 to 2009, Syracuse won the **Big East Tournament** five times, played in the national championship game three times, and won it once.

Boeheim's stars during those *decades* included Dwayne "Pearl" Washington, Leo Rautins, Rafael Addison, Dave Johnson, Sherman Douglas, Rony Seikaly, Derrick Coleman, Stevie Thompson, Billy Owens, Lawrence Moten, John Wallace, Carmelo Anthony, Gerry McNamara, and Hakim Warrick.

Each had the skill to control a game by himself. But Boeheim taught them the secret to winning—playing unselfish **team basketball** and putting Syracuse's goals first.

LEFT: John Wallace soars to the rim for a dunk.
ABOVE: Pearl Washington brings the ball up the court.

21st Century

The excitement of Syracuse basketball continued in the 21st *century*. Jim Boeheim coached his players to 20-win seasons in 2000–01 and 2001–02. Could he keep it up with a young and *inexperienced* team in 2002–03? The answer was yes.

Two freshmen, Carmelo Anthony and Gerry McNamara, proved that a team could win without *experienced* leaders. Anthony and McNamara helped the Orangemen to 30 victories and the national championship in the spring of 2003. They set a new standard for the players who followed them, including Donte Greene, Jonny Flynn, and Demetris Nichols.

Winning championships is great fun for players and students. However, it's a lot of pressure for the coach. Boeheim knows this as well as anyone. Because college players come and go in just a few years, a coach must always be looking for new talent in his **lineup**. He also must teach his players how to work together. Boeheim has done an amazing job. In 2009–10, Syracuse notched its 40th winning season in a row. No college team has ever matched this record.

Carmelo Anthony and Gerry McNamara slap a high-five during Syracuse's championship season in 2002–03.

Home Court

The Orange play their home games in the Carrier Dome. It's the largest domed stadium on any college campus in the United States. The Carrier Dome opened in 1980 and is home to the Syracuse men's and women's basketball teams, as well as the school's football and lacrosse teams.

The Dome is covered with a strong, *fiberglass* fabric that is stretched over 64 different panels. The panels can be heated in the winter so that snow melts as soon as it lands on the roof. The roof, lights, and speakers are held together with steel cables. Sixteen giant fans blow air into the building to keep the Dome inflated.

BY THE NUMBERS

- *The Carrier Dome has nearly 35,000 seats for basketball.*
- *More than 26 million people have gone to events at the Carrier Dome.*
- *As of 2010, Syracuse has retired the jerseys of nine basketball players— Rony Seikaly (4), Vic Hanson (8), Billy Gabor (17), Wilmeth Sidat-Singh (19), Sherman Douglas (20), Dave Bing (22), Billy Owens (30), Pearl Washington (31), and Derrick Coleman (44).*

The Carrier Dome is filled with excited fans for a Syracuse game.

Dressed for Success

Syracuse's original colors were pink and green. The school switched to orange in 1890 and began calling its teams the Orangemen. Some people thought the name referred to the skin color of Native Americans and believed it was ***insulting*** to them. The school eventually changed the name of all its teams to the Orange.

Syracuse has worn many combinations of orange, blue, and white throughout its history. In the 1940s and 1950s, blue and white were the school's main colors, even though the team was known as the Orangemen. Over the years, the school has made orange its most ***prominent*** color. It has become a bit brighter during that time. Blue, on the other hand, is now used mostly as trim. For home games, the team wears a white uniform with ORANGE spelled out in orange. On the road, the team wears an orange uniform with SYRACUSE spelled out in white.

SYRACUSE UNIVERSITY 1988-89
BASKETBALL

DERRICK COLEMAN

Derrick Coleman models the Syracuse home uniform from the late 1980s.

UNIFORM BASICS

The basketball uniform is very simple. It consists of a roomy top and baggy shorts.

- The top hangs from the shoulders, with big "scoops" for the arms and neck. This style has not changed much over the years.

- Shorts, however, have changed a lot. They used to be very short, so players could move their legs freely. In the last 20 years, shorts have gotten longer and much baggier.

Basketball uniforms look the same as they did long ago ... until you look very closely. In the old days, the shorts had belts and buckles. The tops were made of a thick cotton called "jersey," which got very heavy when players sweated. Later, uniforms were made of shiny **satin**. They may have looked great, but they did not "breathe." As a result, players got very hot! Today, most uniforms are made of **synthetic** materials that soak up sweat and keep the body cool.

Jonny Flynn wears the team's all-orange road uniform during a 2008–09 game.

We're Number 1!

Syracuse has finished the basketball season ranked first in the country three times. The first two titles came just eight years apart, in 1917–18 and then again in 1925–26. Back then, there was no tournament to decide the college championship. The best team was picked afterward by a group of experts from an athletic organization known as the Helms Foundation.

The 1917–18 squad was coached by Ed Dollard. It starred Joe Schwarzer and Charles Dolley. Schwarzer was one of the top players in

the nation, but Dolley made the best shot of the year. He broke a 23–23 tie with the University of Pennsylvania when he flung the ball over his head and into the basket from the corner to win the game. Fans swore Dolley never looked at the rim!

When the two teams met again on the last day of the season, Penn won 17–16. So who was the best team in college basketball? The players wanted to decide once and for all on the court with another game, but the Penn coaches would not allow it. Syracuse was later declared the national champion.

For the 1925–26 season, coach Lew Andreas put a great team on the floor. It starred Vic Hanson, Charlie Lee, and Gotch Carr. Once again, Syracuse faced off in a big game against Penn. Both teams were **undefeated** when they met four days after Christmas. Hanson's present to the home fans was the best game of his life. The Orangemen won in **overtime**, 30–25. Hanson scored 25 points—as many as the entire Penn team! Syracuse lost just one game later that season and finished 19–1.

Syracuse fans would have to wait 77 years for their next championship. This

time, the team had to win the NCAA Tournament. When the 2002–03 season began, no one paid much attention to the Orangemen. After Syracuse lost its opening game, some wondered whether the team would even finish the year with a winning record!

Two first-year players—Carmelo Anthony and Gerry McNamara—would have something to say about that. Anthony was a cool,

LEFT: Lew Andreas, the coach that led the 1925–26 team.
ABOVE: Gerry McNamara celebrates a win during the 2002–03 season.

confident forward who was a fantastic scorer and rebounder. McNamara was a tough shooting guard.

Coach Jim Boeheim had total faith in Anthony and McNamara. When the team lost a key player, Boeheim asked McNamara to switch positions and run the offense. He and Anthony teamed with sophomore Hakim Warrick to give Syracuse great energy. As the season wore on, the Orangemen started to believe they could beat anybody.

By the NCAA Tournament, they could. The Orangemen defeated Manhattan College, Oklahoma State, and Auburn. The games were close, but each time a new hero stepped forward to make the winning difference. Syracuse was now one of eight teams left in the tournament. The

Orangemen next faced Oklahoma, one of the top teams in the country. Anthony led Syracuse to an amazing victory, 63–47.

In the Final Four, the Orangemen matched up against Texas. Anthony was unstoppable again. He scored 33 points and grabbed 14 rebounds before hurting his back. Syracuse held on to win, 95–84. The Orangemen were one victory away from the championship. Only Kansas stood in their way.

The Jayhawks **double-teamed** Anthony every chance they got. That left McNamara open. He nailed six **3-pointers** in the first half. Anthony helped his team with passes and rebounds, and Syracuse opened up a big lead.

The teams battled hard for 40 minutes. Syracuse held an 81–78 lead with just a few seconds left. Michael Lee of Kansas had an open 3-pointer to tie the game. As he let his shot go, Warrick came flying through the air to swat it out of bounds and save the game. Syracuse was the national champion!

LEFT: Carmelo Anthony raises his arms in victory after Syracuse's win over Texas.   **ABOVE**: Hakim Warrick stretches to make the game-winning block against Kansas.

Go-To Guys

DANNY SCHAYES   6′ 11″ Center

• BORN: 5/10/1959   • PLAYED FOR VARSITY: 1977–78 TO 1980–81

Danny Schayes was a smooth, graceful player whose father, Dolph, had been a **professional** star in Syracuse. Danny was the team's sixth man for three seasons. When he finally got to start, he led the Orangemen in scoring and rebounding. He was honored as First Team **All-Big East** and an **All-American**.

DWAYNE WASHINGTON   6′ 3″ Guard

• BORN: 1/6/1964   • PLAYED FOR VARSITY: 1983–84 TO 1985–86

Every college team *recruited* playground legend Dwayne Washington when he was in high school. The "Pearl" chose the Orangemen. He was a First Team All-Big East pick every year at Syracuse and a First Team All-American as a junior.

DERRICK COLEMAN   6′ 10″ Forward

• BORN: 6/21/1967   • PLAYED FOR VARSITY: 1986–87 TO 1989–90

Derrick Coleman was an amazing all-around star who had the talent to score 30 points a game. But Syracuse won because "DC" was a team player. His defense, passing, rebounding, and scoring made him the Big East Player of the Year as a senior.

Billy Owens

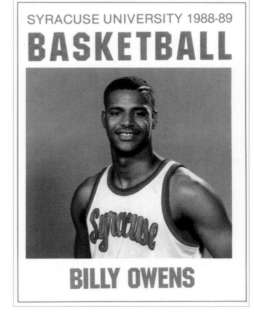

SYRACUSE UNIVERSITY 1988-89
BASKETBALL

BILLY OWENS

BILLY OWENS   6´ 8˝ Forward

- BORN: 5/1/1969
- PLAYED FOR VARSITY: 1988–89 TO 1990–91

One year after Derrick Coleman was named the top player in the Big East, his friend and teammate Billy Owens won the award. Owens did whatever coach Jim Boeheim asked. When Boeheim needed Owens to become a scorer, he averaged 23.2 points per game in 1990–91.

HAKIM WARRICK   6´ 8˝ Forward

- BORN: 7/8/1982   • PLAYED FOR VARSITY: 2001–02 TO 2004–05

Hakim Warrick was named Big East Player of the Year in 2004–05. He was also **Most Valuable Player (MVP)** of the Big East Tournament that season. Warrick will always be remembered for his blocked shot that helped Syracuse win the 2003 national championship.

CARMELO ANTHONY   6´ 8˝ Forward

- BORN: 5/29/1984   • PLAYED FOR VARSITY: 2002–03

Carmelo Anthony played just one year for Syracuse before jumping to the **National Basketball Association (NBA)**. What a year it was! "Melo" averaged 22 points and 10 rebounds per game. He was named the 2003 NCAA Tournament **Most Outstanding Player (MOP)**.

VIC HANSON   5′ 10″ Forward

VIC HANSON   End

- BORN: 7/20/1903   • DIED: 4/10/1982
- PLAYED FOR VARSITY: 1924–25 TO 1926–27

Vic Hanson was captain of the Syracuse football and baseball teams. Yet he was at his very best as a high-scoring star in the early days of basketball. Hanson dribbled, passed, and shot like a modern player. In 1925–26, he set a school record for points and led the team to a 19–1 record.

BILLY GABOR   5′ 11″ Forward

- BORN: 5/13/1922   • PLAYED FOR VARSITY: 1942–43 & 1945–46 TO 1947–48

Billy Gabor was nicknamed "Bullet Billy" because of his speed on the court. He set a school scoring record as a freshman before leaving to fight in World War II. After Gabor returned, he led the squad in scoring three years in a row. He was the first Syracuse player to reach 1,000 points.

DAVE BING   6′ 3″ Guard

- BORN: 11/24/1943   • PLAYED FOR VARSITY: 1963–64 TO 1965–66

Dave Bing was part of a wave of super scorers in college basketball during the 1960s. He averaged 28.4 points per game as a senior. After Bing joined the NBA, he became the first guard in 20 years to lead the league in scoring.

RAFAEL ADDISON   6′ 7″ Guard/Forward

- BORN: 7/22/1964   • PLAYED FOR VARSITY: 1982–83 TO 1985–86

Rafael Addison was nearly impossible for opponents to stop. Guards were too small to cover him and forwards weren't quick enough. His shot was like a guided missile that rarely missed its mark.

LAWRENCE MOTEN   6′ 5″ Guard/Forward

- BORN: 3/25/1972
- PLAYED FOR VARSITY: 1991–92 TO 1994–95

Lawrence Moten was the kind of player that coach Jim Boeheim loved. He could play guard or forward, made few mistakes, and scored on jump shots and **drives** to the basket. Moten averaged over 19 points per game in two seasons and finished as the school's all-time leading scorer.

JOHN WALLACE   6′ 8″ Forward

- BORN: 2/9/1974
- PLAYED FOR VARSITY: 1992–93 TO 1995–96

John Wallace loved the pressure of a big game. As a senior, he led the team in scoring 30 times. Wallace's 3-pointer in the 1996 NCAA Tournament beat Georgia in overtime and helped Syracuse reach the championship game.

LEFT: Vic Hanson
ABOVE: Lawrence Moten

23

ROOSEVELT BOUIE 6´ 11˝ Center

• BORN: 1/21/1958 • PLAYED FOR VARSITY: 1976–77 TO 1979–80

Syracuse players were known as "Roy's Runts" under coach Roy Danforth. After Jim Boeheim took over and recruited Roosevelt Bouie and Louis Orr, the team was called the "Bouie & Louie Show." Bouie was a spectacular defender. The team won 100 games during his career.

LOUIS ORR 6´ 8˝ Forward

• BORN: 5/7/1958

• PLAYED FOR VARSITY: 1976–77 TO 1979–80

Louis Orr was a silky-smooth forward who made basketball look simple. He was at his best when the ball was headed for the basket. Orr always seemed to be in the perfect spot for a rebound.

RONY SEIKALY 6´ 10˝ Center

• BORN: 5/10/1965

• PLAYED FOR VARSITY: 1984–85 TO 1987–88

Rony Seikaly was a powerful rebounder and shot-blocker. When Syracuse reached the **NCAA Final** in 1987, he was the man in the middle for the team. One year later, Seikaly and Derrick Coleman led the squad to victory in the Big East Tournament.

SHERMAN DOUGLAS   6′ 0″ Guard

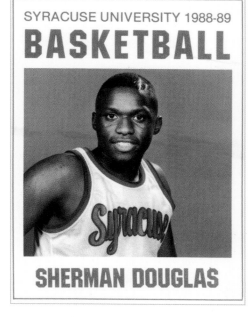

SYRACUSE UNIVERSITY 1988-89
BASKETBALL
SHERMAN DOUGLAS

- BORN: 9/15/1966
- PLAYED FOR VARSITY: 1985–86 TO 1988–89

Fans called Sherman Douglas the "General" because he was a great leader. He played his best in big games. His favorite pass was the **alley-oop**. Douglas had three favorite targets for this play—Derrick Coleman, Rony Seikaly, and Stevie Thompson.

JASON HART   6′ 3″ Guard

- BORN: 4/29/1979   • PLAYED FOR VARSITY: 1996–97 TO 1999–00

Jason Hart and center Etan Thomas gave Syracuse a great defense in the 1990s. They were quick, tough, and fearless. On offense, Hart was a good **playmaker** who drove opponents crazy with his drives to the basket. He also loved to battle bigger players for rebounds.

GERRY McNAMARA   6′ 2″ Guard

- BORN: 8/28/1983   • PLAYED FOR VARSITY: 2002–03 TO 2005–06

Gerry McNamara was a **clutch** player. He loved to have the ball in his hands with the game on the line. As a freshman, "G-Mac" was the point guard on Syracuse's championship team. In 2004, he set a school record with 43 points in an NCAA Tournament game.

LEFT: Derrick Coleman leaps into the arms of Rony Seikaly.
ABOVE: Sherman Douglas

25

On the Sidelines

Syracuse has been playing basketball for more than 100 seasons. During that time, the school had only seven coaches: John Scott, Ed Dollard, Lew Andreas, Marc Guley, Fred Lewis, Roy Danforth, and Jim Boeheim. Dollard led the team to a championship in 1917–18. Andreas also led the team to a national title, in 1925–26. He won 358 games in 27 seasons.

During the 1960s, Lewis brought a high-scoring offense to Syracuse. He was a good recruiter who found talented shooters from all over New York State. Danforth coached his teams to be almost unbeatable at home. He found ways to get the students excited and made basketball fun for his players.

In 1976, Boeheim became Syracuse's coach. He had been with the team since 1963, first as a player and then as an assistant coach. Boeheim turned the Orange into a powerhouse. His secret was changing his *strategy* from year to year to let his players make the most of their skills. Boeheim's teams were most dangerous when he had a smart point guard and athletic forwards. In 2003, the Orange won the national championship under Boeheim. He was elected to the **Basketball Hall of Fame** in 2005 and won his 800th game in 2009.

Jim Boeheim holds up the 2003 NCAA championship trophy.

Rivals

Two important events in 1980 helped create heated *rivalries* for Syracuse. The first was the opening of the Carrier Dome. It was built with seats for more than 30,000 basketball fans. Before that, the team played in a building that held fewer than 10,000 fans. The big crowds at the Carrier Dome helped Syracuse recruit top players. Those stars have given Syracuse fans lots of fond memories in games against the Orange's top rivals.

Also in 1980, Syracuse completed its first season as a member of The Big East Conference. The team finished in first place but lost in the final game of the conference tournament. The school that beat them was Georgetown. That was the beginning of one of the best rivalries in college basketball. The schools would meet for the tournament championship four more times from 1984 to 1992.

In 1990, another fierce rival emerged. This time, the University of Connecticut (UConn) challenged Syracuse for "top dog" in the Big East. Since then, the two teams have been very evenly matched. When the players leave the floor after facing each other, they feel like they played three games instead of one.

Jim Calhoun and Jim Boeheim show off trophies that mark
700 career wins by each coach.

Through 2009, Syracuse was way ahead of UConn in their rivalry. But in the games in which Jim Boeheim coached against Jim Calhoun, their record is almost even. With Boeheim and Calhoun on the sidelines, the Syracuse–UConn rivalry has been the most *intense* in the Big East.

One Great Day

The Big East was only two years old when the 1981 conference tournament began. One year earlier, Syracuse had lost to Georgetown in the final game. Now the Orangemen were playing in front of their hometown fans and students at the Carrier Dome. Syracuse senior Danny Schayes was confident that his team would win. So were super sophomores Tony Bruin, Erich Santifer, and Leo Rautins. They led Syracuse to victory over St. John's and then Georgetown to reach the tournament final, against Villanova.

The two schools battled into overtime. The game was tied after the first extra period and went into a second overtime. Again, neither team could gain an advantage. With eight seconds left in the third overtime, the score was tied, 80–80. Santifer fired a 12-foot jump shot. The Syracuse fans groaned when the ball clanked off the rim. It looked like a fourth overtime was coming.

But wait! The curly head and outstretched arm of Rautins rose toward the rim and tipped the ball in. At the moment when all seemed

Leo Rautins watches his tip-in fall through the hoop to beat Villanova.

lost, the young forward had given his team its first Big East championship. More than 30,000 fans stood and screamed at once. The building felt like it was shaking!

Playing on a sore knee, Rautins was exhausted by the third overtime. But he dug down deep and found just a little bit more strength in his tired body. A few minutes later, he was named MVP of the tournament.

"It showed you something about Leo, for him to get to that ball and tap it in after all that," Bruin said afterward. "It says something about his will."

It Really Happened

hen rivals like Syracuse and Connecticut meet during the regular season, the fans expect a close, action-packed game. When the Orange and Huskies meet at tournament time, things can get even crazier. In 2009, Syracuse took on UConn in the second round of the Big East Tournament. The Orange had a two-game winning streak against the Huskies in the **postseason**.

Syracuse led 71–69 with time running out. But the Huskies tied the score with one second left. Eric Devendorf responded by swishing an amazing 3-pointer for the Orange. But the referees said the basket did not count—the buzzer had gone off before the ball left Devendorf's fingers. The teams returned to their benches and prepared for overtime.

After the end of the first overtime, the score was still tied. Neither team could win in the second overtime—or the third, or the fourth, or the fifth! In each of these extra periods, UConn had the lead, but the Orange fought back. The crowd in New York's Madison Square Garden screamed until their throats were sore. No one there had ever seen a game like this one.

Jonny Flynn glides to the basket for two of his 34 points against UConn.

Finally, in the sixth overtime, Syracuse pulled away to win 127–117. The star of the game for the Orange was Jonny Flynn. He finished with 34 points and played 67 of the game's 70 minutes.

"I have never been prouder of my team than tonight," said coach Jim Boeheim. "That was the greatest game in history!"

Team Spirit

Syracuse students don't need much help to get excited about their basketball team. Few colleges have more fans, and none can pack more into their home court. Visiting teams hate playing in the loud and spacious Carrier Dome.

Over the years, the team's **mascot** has changed several times. For many years, it was Saltine Bill. He was a student dressed as a Native American chief. That choice made sense. Syracuse was sometimes called Salt City, and it was once home to members of the Iroquois nation.

In the 1970s, however, many fans complained that Syracuse's "Saltine Warrior" made fun of a proud people. The school agreed to find a new mascot. Syracuse tried an ancient Roman gladiator, an orange troll, a man in an orange tuxedo, and an orange cowboy called the Dome Ranger. Finally, in 1995, Otto the Orange was chosen as the school's official mascot. Otto is a furry creature shaped like an orange who wears an orange-and-blue Syracuse cap.

Otto never has a problem making friends with Syracuse fans.

Timeline

The basketball season is played from October through March. That means each season takes place at the end of one year and the beginning of the next. In this timeline, the accomplishments of the team are shown by season.

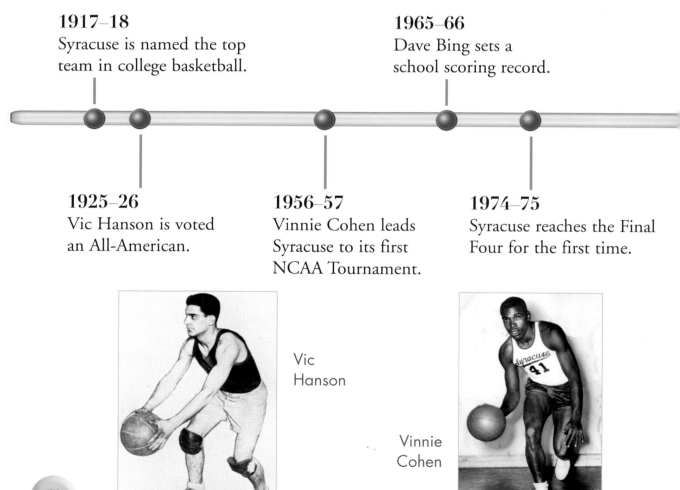

1917–18
Syracuse is named the top team in college basketball.

1965–66
Dave Bing sets a school scoring record.

1925–26
Vic Hanson is voted an All-American.

1956–57
Vinnie Cohen leads Syracuse to its first NCAA Tournament.

1974–75
Syracuse reaches the Final Four for the first time.

Vic Hanson

Vinnie Cohen

The 1987 NCAA
Tournament program

Syracuse coach
Jim Boeheim

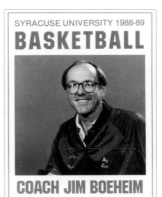

1991–92
The team wins the Big East
Tournament for the third time.

2004–05
The team changes its name
from Orangemen to Orange.

1986–87
Syracuse reaches the
NCAA Tournament final.

2002–03
Syracuse wins the
national championship.

2008–09
Syracuse beats UConn
in six overtimes.

A souvenir
poster of
the 2003
champions

Fun Facts

PITCHING IN

In 1939, one of the top players for Syracuse was Jim Konstanty. He also starred in boxing and soccer. Konstanty's best sport was baseball. In 1950, he was named MVP of the *National League* while playing for the Philadelphia Phillies.

FLYING HIGH

Syracuse's first African-American sports star was Wilmeth Sidat-Singh. He played guard on the basketball team and quarterback on the football team in the 1930s. After graduating, he became a fighter pilot with the famous Tuskegee Airmen in World War II.

SWEET SIXTEEN

Leo Rautins was already an experienced international basketball player when he joined Syracuse in 1980. Rautins was a member of the Canadian National Team at the age of 16!

FRESH FROSH

Carmelo Anthony set a Final Four record for freshmen when he scored 33 points against Texas in 2003. That also set a school record for points by a freshman in a tournament game.

DOUBLE TROUBLE

Vic Hanson was an amazing athlete during his years at Syracuse. He was the first player to enter both the Basketball Hall of Fame and *College Football Hall of Fame*.

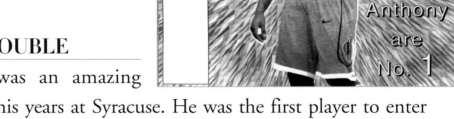

SHOOTING STARS

Bill Smith holds the school record for points in a game. He scored 47 points in a 1971 contest. The first Syracuse player to score at least 40 points was Eddie Miller, in 1951.

LEFT: A trading card of Jim Konstanty **ABOVE**: Carmelo Anthony made headlines with his great performance in the 2003 Final Four.

For the Record

T he great Syracuse teams and players have left their marks on the record books. These are the "best of the best" …

ORANGE AWARD WINNERS

BIG EAST ROOKIE OF THE YEAR		BIG EAST PLAYER OF THE YEAR	
Pearl Washington	1983–84	Derrick Coleman	1989–90
Derrick Coleman	1986–87	Billy Owens	1990–91
Lawrence Moten	1991–92	Hakim Warrick	2004–05
Carmelo Anthony	2002–03		
Jonny Flynn	2007–08*	**BIG EAST DEFENSIVE PLAYER OF THE YEAR**	
		Etan Thomas	1998–99
		Etan Thomas	1999–00
BIG EAST COACH OF THE YEAR			
Jim Boeheim	1983–84	**NCAA TOURNAMENT MOP**	
Jim Boeheim	1990–91	Carmelo Anthony	2002–03
Jim Boeheim	1999–00		

* Shared this honor with another player.

A pennant celebrating the 2003 Final Four.

ORANGE ACHIEVEMENTS

ACHIEVEMENT	YEAR
NCAA Champions	1917–18
NCAA Champions	1925–26
NCAA Final Four	1974–75
Big East Tournament Champions	1980–81
NCAA Finalists	1986–87
Big East Tournament Champions	1987–88
Big East Tournament Champions	1991–92
NCAA Finalists	1995–96
NCAA Champions	2002–03
Big East Tournament Champions	2004–05
Big East Tournament Champions	2005–06

RIGHT: Etan Thomas, the two-time Big East Defensive Player of the Year.
BELOW: Dave Johnson, a star for the 1991–92 team.

The Big East

The Orange are part of the Big East. Syracuse was one of seven schools that formed the conference in 1979. Since then the Big East has grown to 16 schools. These are the Orange's neighbors …

THE BIG EAST

1. Syracuse University Orange
   Syracuse, New York
2. University of Louisville Cardinals
   Louisville, Kentucky
3. Marquette University Golden Eagles
   Milwaukee, Wisconsin
4. University of Connecticut Huskies
   Storrs, Connecticut
5. University of Pittsburgh Panthers
   Pittsburgh, Pennsylvania
6. Villanova University Wildcats
   Villanova, Pennsylvania
7. DePaul University Blue Demons
   Chicago, Illinois
8. Georgetown University Hoyas
   Washington, D.C.
9. West Virginia University Mountaineers
   Morgantown, West Virginia
10. University of Notre Dame Fighting Irish
    South Bend, Indiana
11. University of Cincinnati Bearcats
    Cincinnati, Ohio
12. Providence College Friars
    Providence, Rhode Island
13. St. John's University Red Storm
    Queens, New York
14. Seton Hall University Pirates
    South Orange, New Jersey
15. Rutgers University Scarlet Knights
    New Brunswick, New Jersey
16. University of South Florida Bulls
    Tampa, Florida

The College Game

College basketball may look like the same game you see professional teams play, but there are some important differences. The first is that college teams play half as many games as the pros do. That's because the players have to attend classes, write papers, and study for exams! Below are several other differences between college and pro basketball.

CLASS NOTES

Most college players are younger than pro players. They are student-athletes who have graduated from high school and now play on their school's varsity team, which is the highest level of competition. Most are between the ages of 18 and 22.

College players are allowed to compete for four seasons. Each year is given a different name or "class"—freshman (first year), sophomore (second year), junior (third year), and senior (fourth year). Sometimes highly skilled players leave college before graduation to play in the pros.

RULE BOOK

There are several differences between the rules in college basketball and the NBA. Here are the most important ones: 1) In college, games last 40 minutes. Teams play two 20-minute halves. In the pros, teams play 48-minute games, divided into four 12-minute quarters. 2) In college, players are disqualified after five personal fouls. In the pros, that number is six. 3) In college, the 3-point line is 20′ 9″ from the basket. In the pros, the line is three feet farther away.

WHO'S NUMBER 1?

How is the national championship of basketball decided? At the end of each season, the top teams are invited to play in the NCAA Tournament. The teams are divided into four groups, and the winner of each group advances to the Final Four. The Final Four consists of two semifinal games. The winners then play for the championship of college basketball.

CONFERENCE CALL

College basketball teams are members of athletic conferences. Each conference represents a different part of the country. For example, the Atlantic Coast Conference is made up of teams from up and down the East Coast. Teams that belong to the same conference usually play each other twice—once on each school's home court. Teams also play games outside their conference. Wins and losses in these games do not count in the conference standings. However, they are very important to a team's national ranking.

TOURNAMENT TIME

At the end of the year, most conferences hold a championship tournament. A team can have a poor record and still be invited to play in the NCAA Tournament if it wins the conference tournament. For many schools, this is an exciting "second chance." In most cases, the regular-season winner and conference tournament winner are given spots in the national tournament. The rest of the tournament "bids" are given to the best remaining teams.

Glossary

BASKETBALL WORDS TO KNOW

3-POINTERS—Baskets made from behind the 3-point line.

ALL-AMERICAN—A college player voted as the best at his position.

ALL-AROUND—Good at all parts of the game.

ALL-BIG EAST—An honor given each year to the conference's best players at each position.

ALLEY-OOP—A ball thrown to a teammate as he begins to jump that enables him to dunk before he comes down.

AMATEUR—Playing a sport without being paid.

ASSISTS—Passes that lead to successful shots.

BASKETBALL HALL OF FAME—The museum in Springfield, Massachusetts where the game's greatest players are honored; these players are often called "Hall of Famers."

BIG EAST CONFERENCE—A conference originally created for teams in the Northeast. It has expanded to include teams from the Southeast and Midwest. The Big East began play in 1979.

BIG EAST TOURNAMENT—The competition that decides the champion of the conference.

CLUTCH—Able to perform well under pressure.

DOUBLE-TEAMED—Guarded one player with two players.

DRIVES—Strong moves to the basket.

FINAL FOUR—The term for the last four teams remaining in the NCAA Tournament.

LINEUP—The list of players who are playing in a game.

MOST OUTSTANDING PLAYER (MOP)—The award given each year to the best player in the NCAA Tournament.

MOST VALUABLE PLAYER (MVP)—The award given each year to the best player in a league or conference; also given to the best player in the league or conference tournament.

NATIONAL BASKETBALL ASSOCIATION (NBA)—The professional league that has been operating since 1946–47.

NATIONAL COLLEGIATE ATHLETIC ASSOCIATION (NCAA)—The organization that oversees the majority of college sports.

NCAA FINAL—The last game of the NCAA Tournament; it decides the national champion.

NCAA TOURNAMENT—The competition that determines the champion of college basketball.

OVERTIME—The extra period played when a game is tied after 40 minutes.

PLAYMAKER—Someone who helps his teammates score by passing the ball.

POSTSEASON—A term for games played after the regular season.

PROFESSIONAL—A player or team that plays a sport for money. College players are not paid, so they are considered amateurs.

TEAM BASKETBALL—A style of play that involves everyone on the court instead of just one or two stars.

OTHER WORDS TO KNOW

CENTURY—A period of 100 years.

COLLEGE FOOTBALL HALL OF FAME—The museum in Indiana where college football's greatest players are honored.

DECADES—Periods of 10 years; also specific periods, such as the 1950s.

EXPERIENCED—Having knowledge and skill in a job.

FIBERGLASS—A solid glass material made from a combination of other materials.

INEXPERIENCED—Lacking great knowledge.

INSULTING—Mean or hurtful.

INTENSE—Very strong or very deep.

MASCOT—An animal or person believed to bring a group good luck.

NATIONAL LEAGUE—The older of baseball's two major leagues; it began play in 1876.

PROMINENT—Major or easy to notice.

RECRUITED—Competed for a student-athlete. Each year colleges recruit the best high school players and offer them athletic scholarships.

RIVALRIES—Extremely emotional competitions.

SATIN—A smooth, shiny fabric.

STRATEGY—A plan or method for succeeding.

SYNTHETIC—Made in a laboratory, not in nature.

TRADITION—A belief or custom that is handed down from generation to generation.

UNDEFEATED—Without a loss.

Places to Go

ON THE ROAD

SYRACUSE ORANGE
900 Irving Avenue
Syracuse, New York 13244
(315) 443-2702

NAISMITH MEMORIAL BASKETBALL HALL OF FAME
1000 West Columbus Avenue
Springfield, Massachusetts 01105
(877) 4HOOPLA

ON THE WEB

THE SYRACUSE ORANGE
 * *Learn more about the Orange*

suathletics.syr.edu

BIG EAST CONFERENCE
 * *Learn more about The Big East Conference teams*

www.bigeast.org

THE BASKETBALL HALL OF FAME
 * *Learn more about history's greatest players*

www.hoophall.com

ON THE BOOKSHELF

To learn more about the sport of basketball, look for these books at your library or bookstore:
 * Labrecque, Ellen. *Basketball*. Ann Arbor, Michigan: Cherry Lake Publishing, 2009.
 * Porterfield, Jason. *Basketball in the Big East Conference*. New York, New York: Rosen Central, 2008.
 * Stewart, Mark and Kennedy, Mike. *Swish: the Quest for Basketball's Perfect Shot*. Minneapolis, Minnesota: Millbrook Press, 2009.

Index

PAGE NUMBERS IN **BOLD** REFER TO ILLUSTRATIONS.

About the Author

MARK STEWART has written more than 30 books on basketball players and teams, and over 100 sports books for kids. He has also interviewed dozens of athletes, politicians, and celebrities. Mark grew up in New York City and was a big NBA fan. One of his favorite players was Dave Bing, who played for the Detroit Pistons in the 1970s. Years later, when Bing became mayor of Detroit, Mark wrote an Internet biography of the former Syracuse star. Mark comes from a family of writers. His grandfather was Sunday Editor of *The New York Time*s and his mother was Articles Editor for *Ladies' Home Journal* and *McCall's*. Mark became interested in sports during lazy summer days spent at the Connecticut home of his father's godfather, sportswriter John R. Tunis. Mark is a graduate of Duke University, with a degree in History. He lives with his wife Sarah, and daughters Mariah and Rachel, overlooking Sandy Hook, New Jersey.

MATT ZEYSING is the resident historian at the Basketball Hall of Fame in Springfield, Massachusetts. His research interests include the origins of the game of basketball, the development of professional basketball in the first half of the 20th century, and the culture and meaning of basketball in American society.

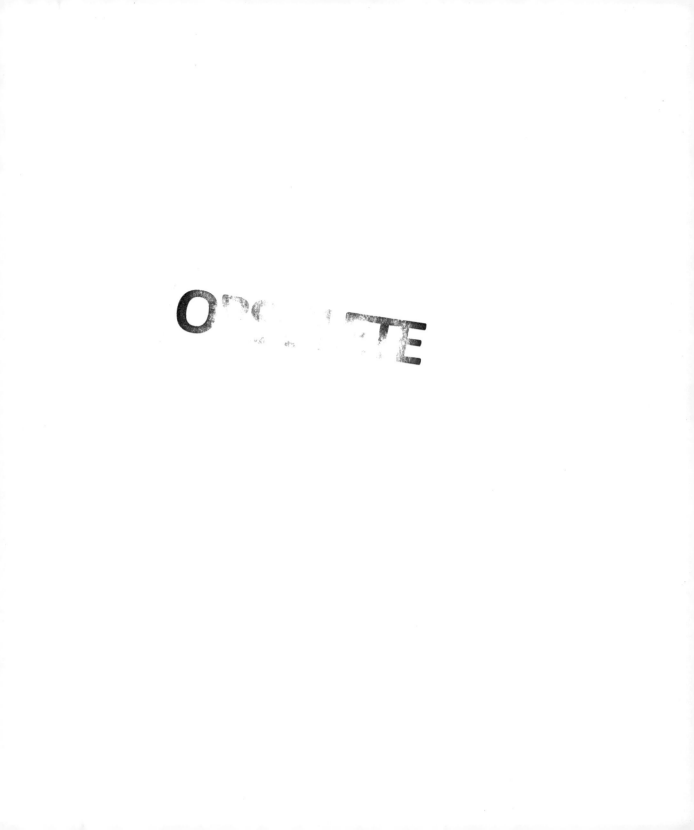

OBSOLETE